ACTIVISM IN ACTION
······ A HISTORY ······™

THE FIGHT FOR THE
ENVIRONMENT

PHILIP WOLNY

New York

For Lucy and Amanda

Published in 2020 by The Rosen Publishing Group, Inc.
29 East 21st Street, New York, NY 10010

Library of Congress Cataloging-in-Publication Data

Names: Wolny, Philip, author.
Title: The fight for the environment / Philip Wolny.
Description: First edition. | New York, NY : Rosen Publishing
Group, 2020. | Series: Activism in Action: A History | Includes
bibliographical references and index.
Identifiers: LCCN 2018016611| ISBN 9781508185505 (library
bound) | ISBN 9781508185499 (pbk.)
Subjects: LCSH: Environmentalism—History—Juvenile litera-
ture.
Classification: LCC GE195.5 .W65 2020 | DDC 333.72—dc23
LC record available at https://lccn.loc.gov/2018016611

Manufactured in China

On the cover: Activists fight for the environment in various
ways, such as by participating in Earth Day events around the
world (*top*) and partnering with like-minded volunteers to rid
our coastlines of debris (*bottom*).

CONTENTS

INTRODUCTION

About 41 miles (66 kilometers) off the Louisiana coast in the Gulf of Mexico, the Deepwater Horizon oil rig was leased to BP (British Petroleum) and had a crew of more than one hundred. On the evening of April 20, 2010, a massive gas explosion killed eleven workers, injured seventeen more, and began the worst maritime oil spill in history. Thousands of square miles of ocean were affected, with massive amounts of oil washing up on Gulf shores. Marine life was imperiled, and the livelihoods of fishermen and shrimpers were affected for months, as more than a third of all government-controlled waters were closed. Oil workers also suffered because a moratorium put a stop to oil drilling in the region.

The BP oil spill was just one example of the environmental and economic damage that can occur when hunting for fossil fuels. The destruction angered many longtime activists who were dedicated to fighting for and pro-tecting the environment for current and future generations. It also angered newer, younger activists who were ready to speak up and take action for the environment. Energized, they pulled together in their activism.

United States Fish and Wildlife Service biologists catch a pelican for cleaning in June 2010 in the aftermath of the massive BP Deepwater Horizon oil spill in the Gulf of Mexico earlier that year.

Environmental activism has a long and rich history, with many people and organizations working in different ways to gain ground. Scientists and those studying climate change try to convince governments to end destructive policies and to encourage businesses, including oil, gas, and coal companies, to pollute less. Protesters try to prevent new pipelines and other possibly damaging projects from being built. One such example is the famous Dakota Access Pipeline protest, staged by indigenous Native American activists and their allies. Beginning in 2016, hundreds (and sometimes thousands) of activists participated in sit-ins to protect the water supplies of the Standing Rock Indian Reservation. Many were attacked and injured by law enforcement agents and private security contractors, while others were charged for crimes—unfairly, according to environmentalists and human rights groups.

Throughout the world, organizations like Greenpeace, the Sierra Club, and the National Audubon Society use their political influence and the support from millions to make a difference for the environment. At the same time, smaller, more aggressive activist groups work at the grassroots level, protesting projects they think will endanger their cities, towns, and neighborhoods. Newer environmental activists, especially in the so-called Global South, represent communities and people in the poorer, more developing nations of Africa, Asia, and South America. They use more radical and innovative efforts to expand the environmental movement and tackle local concerns that

challenge governments, businesses, and communities to do better.

From fighting the causes of climate change,
to changing government and corporate policies,
to putting their bodies on the line, environmental
activists have made great strides and worldwide
headlines. As they work tirelessly to help save our
planet, let us take a look at where the fight for the
environment began, how it has developed, and
where it will take us as the stakes grow even higher.

CHAPTER ONE

EARLY ENVIRONMENTALISM

P eople have sought to preserve, restore, and improve their natural environment for as far back as history records. Ancient civilizations, from the Greeks to the Indians and Chinese, have felt compelled to protect the natural world. One of the earliest environmentally minded projects was waste disposal. Early peoples did not need to feel a kinship with the earth to know that getting rid of sewage—wastewater and human excrement—was in everyone's best interest. As populations grew, sewage and garbage began filling the streets. Overcrowding and uncontrolled waste resulted in community-wide illnesses.

Among the earliest recyclers were the ancient Romans, who reused glass, and ancient Egyptians, who repurposed letters and legal documents made from papyrus into burial wrappings for mummies. Ancient Romans, however, were of the mind that humans should dominate the world around them. They believed that nature's best use was to improve human lives and conditions, and protecting animals and the environment

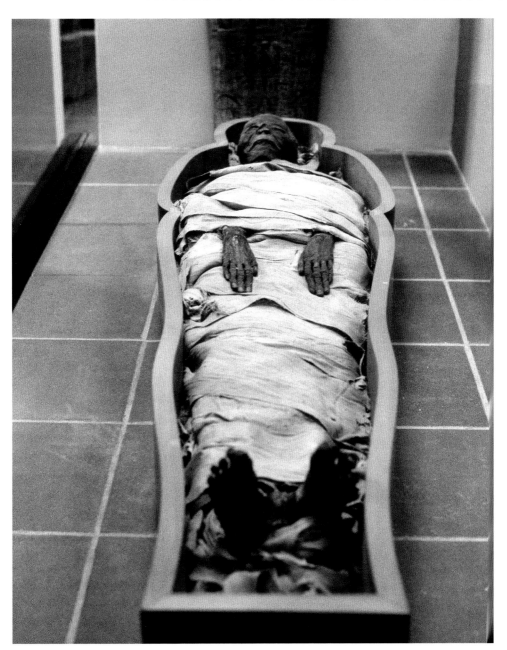

One might not connect ancient Egyptian mummies, like this one at the Vatican Museum, with recycling, but many historians now believe at least some wrappings for the dead included repurposed materials.

was a secondary concern. Some scientists and writers, like population biologist Paul. R. Ehrlich and his wife, author Anne H. Ehrlich, point out that Rome paid for its attitude toward the environment. They wrote in *Mother Earth News*, "The Romans hit hard at their environment ... but it struck back! Deforestation, the depletion of soils, and the exhaustion of mines were all factors in the fall of Rome's Empire."

ROMANTICISM AND THE BIRTH OF CONSERVATION

A movement called Romanticism took shape from the second half of the eighteenth century and into the nineteenth. It began mostly in Europe as a reaction to the uncertainties sparked by the Industrial Revolution, a period of time in which machines mass produced goods. Many people were nervous about the growth of factories, its noise, and the inhumanity of mass production and other phenomena of the industrial era, including pollution and deforestation. Plus, coal-fired factories spewed toxic smoke into the air, reaching hundreds of cities and towns across England. Romanticism moved away from this and towards emotion and individuality. It encouraged a love of nature, rooted in nostalgia for the past.

The movement affected intellectual thought, literature, and the creative arts. Romantic writers idealized the unspoiled wilderness, and artists featured natural landscapes of mountains, hills, and forests.

The pollution of the Industrial Revolution also affected the United States as it grew into an industrial power. Movements aimed at social and political reform were established in the nineteenth century, including a conservation movement to preserve natural beauty. In her writings for the National Park Service (NPS), Ann E. Chapman described three types of conservation that environmental historians say arose in the 1800s: utilitarian, preservationist, and wildlife habitats. Utilitarian conservation protected natural resources because it was the smart thing to do and it offered short- and long-term benefits. Preservationist conservation protected the scenic beauty of nature for everyone's enjoyment. Wildlife habitats protected natural areas for animals and plants.

THE FIRST "ENVIRONMENTALISTS"

Many nineteenth-century environmentalists—as we understand the philosophy and movement today—were scientists, writers, and other intellectual leaders. Diplomat and scholar George Perkins March wrote one of the earliest books on conservation in 1864, entitled *Man and Nature: Or, Physical Geography as Modified by Human Action*. Marsh's book discussed deforestation, as well as soil erosion and flooding, that arose from farming, hunting, and waste disposal. According to the NPS, "A key idea that came out Marsh's work—that forests were important for watershed protection—provided a strong rationale for forest conservation initiatives in the latter half of the 19th and first part of the 20th centuries."

Another major environmentalist of the era was John Muir, a former inventor who became one of America's most famous naturalists and conservationists. Muir walked cross-country from Indianapolis, Indiana, to the Gulf of Mexico, and later lived alone in California's Yosemite Valley and the Sierra Nevada mountains. He also explored the American Southwest, the Pacific Northwest, and Alaska. Muir pressed the US government to conserve large chunks of land, and in 1890, was instrumental in helping to set up Yosemite National Park and Sequoia National Park. Two years later, Muir founded the Sierra Club in San Francisco, California, a group he led as president. Its earliest efforts included pushing for the legal protection of wilderness areas, mapping them out, and organizing hikes and climbs.

AUDUBON SOCIETIES

Although women would not have the right to vote until 1920, they were far from being politically powerless. The reform movements of the time helped to bring women together, especially those who were interested in birding and ornithology (the scientific study of birds). Dozens of species were nearly wiped out, or made extinct altogether, due to the feathered hat fashion trend. Boston socialite Harriet Lawrence Hemenway enlisted her cousin, Minna B. Hall, in a campaign to get women to boycott the trend. She hosted tea times for her wealthy and influential friends, and thanks to the support of her husband (a shipping heir named Augustus Hemenway), she used their shared contacts as the basis for the Massachusetts Audubon Society. The organization, founded in 1896, helped to protect wildlife and wilderness. Hundreds of women joined, and many led local chapters. Their efforts bore fruit in 1897 when a Massachusetts law outlawed the trade in wild bird feathers. (In 1990, a federal law was passed banning the interstate shipping of animals killed illegally, wherever they were.) According to the NPS, thirty-five states had an Audubon group by 1901. By 1905, the National Audubon Society was set up to coordinate activities and streamline resources.

The four women in this 1915 portrait were among the many who gravitated toward the trend in feathered hats, sparking a movement to spare birds from being killed for their production.

THE NATIONAL PARKS

In the early twentieth century, one of the most important figures pressing conservation was US president Theodore (Teddy) Roosevelt. He was a progressive, reform-minded naturalist, author, and outdoorsman. Although national parks had been established before his presidency (1901–1909), such as Wyoming's Yellowstone (1872) and California's Sequoia (1890) and Yosemite (1890), Roosevelt doubled the protected federal lands, such as national parks and monuments. He also created the United States Forest Service in 1905. According to the NPS, Roosevelt shared the following at the 1908 Conference on the Conservation of Natural Resources:

> We have become great because of the lavish use of our resources. But the time has come to inquire seriously what will happen when our forests are gone, when the coal,

ALICE HAMILTON: ANTILEAD CRUSADER

At the turn of the twentieth century, Alice Hamilton (1869–1970) made a name for herself while studying the effects of industrial diseases, especially chemical exposure on workers. Hamilton spearheaded research into lead, which was proven to be extremely harmful to humans, as well as mercury and other toxins. She helped run a commission on occupational diseases in Illinois, and was involved in federal and state health investigations for more than ten years. She also publicized the dangers of toxic chemicals on industrial workers.

Hamilton was arguably the most important voice in the efforts to get companies to stop using lead, namely in gasoline for automobiles. She testified in 1925 that oil and car companies should work to remove lead. While it took some time, her vision was eventually realized when leaded gas was banned for good in the United States in 1990. Hamilton also became the first female professor at Harvard in 1919, when she served as an assistant professor at Harvard Medical School.

Influential early American toxicologist Alice Hamilton is shown here in 1935 at Hull House in Chicago, where middle-class volunteers lived among the poor to assist them.

the iron, the oil, and the gas are exhausted, when the soils have still further impoverished and washed into the streams, polluting the rivers, denuding the fields and obstructing navigation.

A SAND COUNTY ALMANAC

The United States' new federal highway system—made possible by the Federal-Aid Highway Act of 1956—made cars and commuting more popular than

Landfills all over the world, like this one of discarded computers, create dangerous health and environmental conditions for anyone who lives near them.

ever. City dwellers moved into the suburbs, and a dynamic consumer society became the norm in much of the country and western world. This meant more products, more waste, more gasoline, and, ultimately, a throwaway society.

Several books inspired readers to seriously consider the looming future their world faced with a throwaway society. One such book was *A Sand County Almanac, And Sketches Here and There* (1949), by environmentalist and forester Aldo Leopold. Leopold began his forestry career in 1909, working in Arizona and New Mexico. In his book, he included stories about his farm in Wisconsin, observations and descriptions of nature, and his "land ethic" idea: that there is a balance among people, living things, and the land they both live on, and how people can manage that balance responsibly. Leopold spoke against treating the land and natural things as commodities to be owned, bought, and sold.

Initially, *A Sand County Almanac, And Sketches Here and There* failed to attract much attention, but when it came out in paperback in the 1970s, interest in environmentalism exploded. Leopold's book was highly influential in promoting "deep ecology," the belief that the natural world and all the creatures in it were as important on their own, without considering their benefit to human beings.

THE ECHO PARK DAM CONTROVERSY

An early milestone of environmental activism was the Echo Park Dam affair. In the late 1940s, the federal government decided to dam parts of the upper Colorado River, as well as the Gunnison and Green Rivers, to provide cheaper hydroelectric power for the booming region. Opposition arose from organizations such as

A kayaker enjoys a paddle near the old proposed Echo Park dam site in Dinosaur National Monument in Colorado.

the NPS. Especially controversial were the plans to establish Echo Park Dam within the federally protected Dinosaur National Monument in north-western Colorado.

Conservation writers, including *Harper's* magazine columnist Bernard DeVoto, and a retired officer of the US Army Corps of Engineers, Ulysses S. Grant III, voiced enough opposition through articles and statements that the decision on the dam was delayed for some time. However, the Department of the Interior under President Dwight D. Eisenhower decided to approve the plan in 1953. A chorus of voices stood against them, including conservation-minded groups like the Wilderness Society, the Sierra Club, the Audubon Society, and the Isaak Walton League. The fight against the Echo Park Dam took place largely within the pages of important newspapers, which the assorted anti-dam groups used to great effect, keeping the controversy in the public eye. The Sierra Club's executive director, David Brower, made films about Echo Park, and had Howard Zahniser of the Wilderness Society screen them for congressmen in Washington, DC. Environmental activists also made allies with lawmakers in western states, including California. In 1955, their efforts succeeded, and the dam was removed from a larger development plan.

NEW AWAKENINGS

After World War II ended in 1945, the United States and Soviet Union engaged in the political standoff known as the Cold War (1947–1991). Both were armed with thousands of nuclear weapons, and while they didn't directly attack each other, the global fear was that a minor conflict between the two would escalate into nuclear war, which would destroy the planet. This threat sparked the beginnings of an antinuclear movement. Included in the movement was the Campaign for Nuclear Disarmament, established in 1957 in the United Kingdom. It advocated for civil disobedience and nonviolent resistance, protest strategies used mainly by human rights and civil rights movements led in India by Gandhi and in the United States by Martin Luther King Jr. The use of these strategies by antinuclear activists later influenced protests by environmental activists.

RACHEL CARSON JUMP-STARTS A MOVEMENT

Marine biologist Rachel Carson (1907–1964) had always been interested in nature, especially the sea. She was already an accomplished scientist and science writer when her 1951 book, *The Sea Around Us*, became a bestseller and critical hit. However, it was *Silent Spring* (1962) that made her an influential voice for the environment. Carson spent more than five years researching the toxic effects of everyday chemicals, including dichlorodiphenyltrichloroethane (DDT), a widely used insecticide. She examined what these toxins had done to the environment, and detailed the results in *Silent Spring*. Besides warning about DDT and other toxins, the book introduced the general public to a pressing concern that, if not dealt with, would become a grave emergency. Carson also highlighted the dishonesty of corporations and elected public officials who had hidden or ignored the potential dangers of these substances.

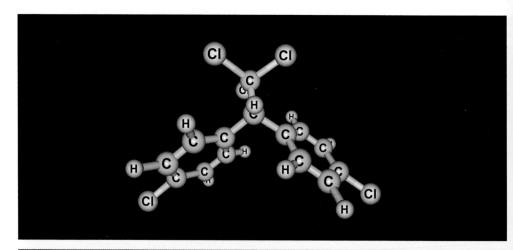

This graphic represents the makeup of dichlorodiphenyltrichloroethane (DDT), a widely used and later outlawed pesticide. The campaign against DDT was a pivotal battle in environmentalism.

Silent Spring elicited public outrage and demands for action. Meanwhile, the pesticide industry and others attacked Carson, criticizing her findings as "hysterical"—taking advantage of a common and ugly sexist stereotype often used against women. But US president John F. Kennedy charged the President's Science Advisory Committee to investigate Carson's claims and the issues she raised. According to the Natural Resources Defense Council (NRDC), Carson's biggest legacy was "a new public awareness that nature was vulnerable to human intervention ... The public debate moved quickly from whether pesticides were dangerous to which ones were dangerous." She had changed the public conversation, and while it took some time, DDT was effectively banned for use in the United States in 1972.

Carson's writings, especially *Silent Spring*, highlighted for the public their very real and delicate connection to nature. It noted how living in balance with nature is crucial for humanity, making it impossible to talk about technology and "progress" without also acknowledging their downsides. Overall, there are few books that are more famous or impactful in the history of environmentalism than Carson's *Silent Spring*.

CHAPTER TWO

THE MODERN ENVIRONMENTAL MOVEMENT

The 1960s and 1970s were a time of great progress for the environmental movement. Activists pressured the public and private sectors about environmental issues, and strides were made in legislation. After the monumental publication of Rachel Carson's *Silent Spring*, biologist Paul R. Ehrlich published the bestseller, *The Population Bomb*, in 1968. Ehrlich, who cowrote the book with his wife, Anne Ehrlich, feared huge social unrest and catastrophic problems on a planet that could no longer support its overpopulation.

These books, as well as an increasing number of warnings about environmental destruction, found the receptive ear of the public. The 1960s was a decade when millions marched for civil rights and when the passion of the antiwar movement split a new, politically engaged generation from that of their parents. The books primed the new generation to aggressively challenge the status quo on energy, agriculture, and other environmental issues.

VETERAN ENVIRONMENTAL GROUPS OF THE TWENTIETH CENTURY

The foundation for a newer environmental movement had been laid over the past decades, allowing important groups to grow in membership and influence, including:

- The Sierra Club: Founded in 1892, it is usually acknowledged as the first true environmental group.
- The Isaak Walton League: Formed in 1922 by recreational fishermen and named after a famous seventeenth century "father of flyfishing," Izaak Walton, the league fought for laws that would preserve clean water. Initially, they saw little success but pushed for minor reforms against water pollution in the 1940s and 1950s.
- The Wilderness Society: Formed in 1935 by Aldo Leopold, Bob Marshall of the United States Forest Service, Brenton MacKaye (who founded the Appalachian Trail), and others, the Wilderness Society has been a formidable force for the preservation of wild places, and those used recreationally by humans. The group's former executive director was the main writer of the

(continued on the next page)

(continued from the previous page)

Wilderness Act of 1964. It provided a legal definition of the word "wilderness" and preserved more than 9 million acres (approximately 3.6 million hectares) of territory that same year.

• The Nature Conservancy, founded in 1951 as a new version of the older Ecological Society of America (1915), is a nonprofit specializing in conservation and biodiversity. It maintains more than 1,500 privately owned nature preserves around the world, along with thousands of miles of rivers.

Thousands of activists turned out for this march opposing rain forest destruction in Tasmania, Australia, in June 2004.

AN ONGOING EMERGENCY

In 1905, English doctor Harold Des Veaux coined the word "smog" to better describe the way London's fog mixed with factory and household smoke. By the 1960s, cities in the United States and elsewhere were also experiencing smog, which could be lethal on especially hot days in places like Los Angeles, California. Industrial wastes polluting the Cuyahoga River in Cleveland, Ohio, were so concentrated that the river caught fire—and not for the first time! It attracted international media attention, much like the gigantic oil spill off the coast of Santa Barbara, California, in January 1969. Both incidents—along with the alarming news about species nearly going extinct due to DDT spraying, including America's national symbol, the bald eagle—galvanized public opinion. Citizens demanded that the government do something, and radical student movements fed the growing environmental movement. One group, Friends of the Earth, formed in 1969 as an antinuclear group. It was headed by David Brower, a former mountaineer and leader of the Sierra Club, who had worked on the Echo Park Dam campaign.

Firefighters battle the fire that erupted from debris in an oil slick on the Cuyahoga River in Cleveland, Ohio, in November 1952.

EARTH DAY, 1970: A WATERSHED MOMENT

Inspired partly by big musical gatherings like Woodstock, environmental activists decided to organize a large meeting and festival. The original idea was that of US senator Gaylord Nelson of Wisconsin, who had been moved by the Santa Barbara oil spill. Nelson saw that the environment would draw impassioned activism, much like the civil rights and antiwar movements had. He and many others teamed up to declare a single day (April 22, 1970), which was dedicated to thousands of "teach-ins" in colleges, high schools, and other venues across the United States.

Several other organizers had a similar idea and became involved in Earth Day, including peace activist John McConnell. It was McConnell who designed the Earth Flag based on the first pictures of the planet captured by space explorers. The main organizer of the actual day's events was Denis Hayes, handpicked by Senator Nelson. Hayes met with students and organizers who helped publicize the day's activities, including one of the largest rallies to take place in New York. They even got New York mayor John Lindsay to provide Central Park as a venue, and to close the city's Fifth Avenue, further spreading word to national media about it.

Across the United States, people hit the streets, public parks, and community centers to figure out ways to help. Conservationists, wildlife defenders, and already engaged groups that were protesting nuclear plants, dirty factories and energy plants, and waste dumping, met up at these rallies. Together, they forged strong alliances and enhanced their collective efforts. With so many likeminded people in attendance, it was inevitable that groups would form. One example was Ecology Action, a prominent and influential volunteer group from Berkeley, California—an epicenter known for its student antiwar efforts and other liberal organizing. Ecology Action spearheaded recycling efforts, and encouraged young, impassioned activists to collect bottles and cans, and push cities, businesses, and individuals to recycle.

Earth Day, and the actions that spun out of it, is very bipartisan. Enthusiastic supporters from both sides of the political aisle continue to work together to save the planet, including students, scientists, people of all economic backgrounds, wilderness and hunting enthusiasts, labor leaders, and farmers.

Children listen to a presentation from NASA members during one of the many thousands of events held during Earth Day in 2016.

GOVERNMENT GETS INVOLVED

US government involvement in environmental preservation dates back to the nineteenth century, with the Rivers and Harbors Act being the oldest federal law on the books. Congress passed it in 1899, banning the polluting of navigable waters without a permit. It also restricted other activities, barring a permit or approval, including damming streams and rivers, and excavating, filling, or changing ports, harbors, and other waterways.

A WAVE OF LEGISLATION

At the end of the 1960s, there were different and often conflicting laws regarding environmental regulation in many states. US president Richard Nixon and others in his administration decided to take elements from different departments to create a larger framework that would fix and enforce these laws. Thus was born the Environmental Protection Agency (EPA), which was signed into existence by Nixon in 1970.

The EPA's main job, at least initially, was to administrate and enforce the measures of the Clean Air Act, originally passed in 1963, but strengthened and improved in 1970. It mandated that states and cities kept levels of certain chemicals, such as sulfur dioxide, lead, and carbon monoxide, at certain levels, or risk fines and penalties.

The Nixon administration continued with its efforts by passing the Clean Water Act in 1972. It was a major revision of an older and less effective law, the Federal Water Pollution Control Act of 1948. According to the EPA's website, some of the 1972 amendments:

- Regulated pollution in US waters
- Gave the EPA the authority to control pollution via measures such as industry wastewater restrictions
- Set requirements for water quality standards for all contaminants
- Made it illegal for individuals to pollute waters
- Funded the building of sewage treatment facilities

A third and important component of the new wave of legislation was the Endangered Species Act, formulated by Congress with the assistance of government scientists and conservationists, and signed into law by Nixon in December 1973. It charged the government with conserving all species of plants and animals that are endangered in their native habitats. This included penalties for groups and individuals who killed members of these species.

GREENPEACE: DIRECT ACTION ON THE HIGH SEAS

One of the models for future environmental groups was the Canadian-born Greenpeace. The group, now a household name, was formed by antiwar activists in 1971 in opposition to a proposed nuclear test on the Alaskan island of Amchitka. Opponents said US military plans to set off a bomb would not only poison and expose the island and nearby areas to radiation, but could also cause a tidal wave. Those protesting the test called themselves the Don't Make a Wave Committee. With help from the Sierra Club, the group chartered a boat and sailed it into the test zone to force the United States to delay or cancel the testing. The name Greenpeace was soon adopted, inspired by the generational peace sign that was a common greeting among the counterculture generation.

Greenpeace soon extended its reach by interfering with whaling, fishing, and hunting they felt was cruel, illegal, or threatened endangered species. Where they could, they photographed and even recorded their actions, both to keep them

Four of the founders of Greenpeace (*left to right*), Jim Bohlen, John Cormack, Irving Stowe, and Paul Côté, are shown here in Vancouver, British Columbia, before an antinuclear protest.

safe and publicize their causes. Over time, Greenpeace used several boats with crews to protest the actions of governments and private industry. A 1973 expedition to block nuclear testing on the French-owned Pacific island of Mururoa ended up with Greenpeace crew members badly beaten by French sailors. Others died when boats capsized, sunk, or encountered bad weather.

Fernando Pereira, a freelance photographer, was killed when a Greenpeace ship, the *Rainbow Warrior*, was bombed on July 10, 1985. It was later revealed that secret agents of the French government had orchestrated the bombing to prevent its use in protests of nuclear testing at Mururoa. The backlash against the French was harsh, and forced the government to criminally charge and convict the agents involved. The agents claimed they only intended to destroy the boat, and did not

LOVE CANAL: A DISASTER SPURS ACTION

In Love Canal, a neighborhood in Niagara Falls, New York, a decades-old waste disposal site made the news in 1978. More than one hundred homes became chemically contaminated, due to nearby chemical drum containers that leaked hazardous waste into the soil. The drums were left behind when the Hooker Chemical Company sold the land two decades earlier to the city for one dollar. The drums rose out of the earth, leaving trees and gardens blackened and dying, and causing the air to stink of toxins. Even worse, according to the

EPA, "Children returned from play with burns on their hands and faces," and the contaminants were widely blamed for high rates of miscarriages and several cases of birth defects. For years, residents lived in fear of heightened cancer rates, due to the carcinogens around them. Many inspectors and safety professionals agreed it was one of the worst examples of industrial pollution they had ever seen.

Many environmentalists were awakened and inspired to take action as a result of Love Canal, and it became a symbol of corporate neglect and greed at the expense of everyday citizens. President Jimmy Carter approved emergency federal help to Love Canal for evacuations and relocation. Nearly a year after the disaster, Carter requested $1.6 billion from Congress to fund a cleanup at Love Canal and future sites. This legislation—known as the Comprehensive Environmental Response, Compensation, and Liability Act (CERCLA)—became known as the Superfund. The Superfund helped decontaminate hundreds of sites nationwide, while helping victims rebuild their lives. According to the EPA's website, there are more than 1,184 sites remaining on the National Priorities List of the EPA, which administers the program, with fifty-two more sites that are proposed.

know a passenger would be on board when they planted the explosives.

CHALLENGES FOR THE MOVEMENT

As people questioned government and society in the 1960s and 1970s, a more aggressive environmentalism emerged. This meant forcing the government to regulate industries that polluted the earth, such as energy and fossil fuel companies, manufacturers, and others that dumped toxins into waterways or buried them in remote areas. With this new focus, there was backlash from the industries that found themselves under government regulations. Resistance was directed at the government itself, and at the activists who pushed for legislation.

Economic problems and hardship plagued the United States and other nations during the 1970s, including several oil crises. President Jimmy Carter, in office from 1977 through 1981, was a strong environmentalist. He encouraged Americans to conserve energy, and thought that if we were truly entering an age when resources were becoming scarce, it only made sense to use less oil, put on a sweater instead of turning up the thermostat, and invest in public transportation.

US president Jimmy Carter holds a press briefing on the roof of the White House in Washington, DC, to show off new solar panels.

However, many Americans were not ready to hear that their own actions (or inaction) were part of the problem.

The movement faced another obstacle when President Ronald Reagan was elected in 1980. Many environmental and safety regulations were rolled back, and a hands-off approach to business regulation was favored. Job creation and business interests became more of a priority than environmental concerns. While environmentalists could count on Carter as an ally, few expected that of Reagan. On June 20, 1979, Carter had installed thirty-two solar panels in the White House to heat water for the building. It was also a government test run for future solar projects, and Carter felt the president should lead by example. When Reagan came into office, he cut most of the funding for research and development into renewable energies like solar and wind power. According to *Scientific American*, in 1986 the Reagan administration "quietly dismantled the White House solar panel installation while resurfacing the roof."

CHAPTER THREE

FIGHTING FOR THE PLANET

F or environmental activists in the United States, the 1980s presented its own set of challenges. Two terms of Ronald Reagan followed by a third from his vice president, George H. W. Bush, meant a federal government skeptical of environmental causes. Nevertheless, some major campaigns were sparked during this era, both by established groups and grassroots organizations.

COMMUNITIES FIGHTING BACK

Among the most important developments were the campaigns for environmental justice and against environmental racism. Begun in the 1970s, activists ramped up these movements in the Reagan era and after. According to the EPA, environmental justice refers to the "fair treatment and meaningful involvement of all people regardless of race, color, national origin, or income,

This view of smokestacks belching out pollution in the Akademichesky district of Moscow, Russia, is a reminder of how cities and industry contribute to worldwide greenhouse gas emissions.

with respect to the development, implementation, and enforcement of environmental laws, regulations, and policies."

Plainly stated, the movement meant to correct inequalities that many poor communities, especially communities of color, had to suffer when it came to environmental hazards. For people in disadvantaged neighborhoods, for example, this meant living near sewage treatment plants, landfills, power plants, industrial facilities, incinerators, and other polluters. People with low socioeconomic statuses often live in places where the air quality is poor, the land and water are toxic, and rates of cancer and other health conditions are significantly higher than those of wealthier areas. Since people in disadvantaged neighborhoods tend to have low funds, they typically have fewer resources and even less of a voice in improve environmental conditions. Whenever a new facility is planned, one that will likely cause harm to a community, it is often placed in an economically distressed area. In many places, the poorest are often people of color, and the issue is referred to as environmental racism. Examples include West Virginians living in one of the most polluted states, and poor Latino city dwellers in Chicago, Illinois, living next to a garbage dump.

THE BIRTH OF ENVIRONMENTAL JUSTICE

Perhaps the first major, publicized environmental justice action of its kind took place in Warren County, North Carolina. In 1978, the state government tried to dispose of 60,000 tons (54,431 metric tons) of contaminated soil. The earth had absorbed 31,000 gallons (117,347 liters) of polychlorinated biphenyl, also known as PCB, and other toxins. The culprit turned out to be the

Ward Transformer Company, which had secretly dumped transformer oil to avoid the expense of safely disposing of it. The toxic soil had to be moved to a landfill, but where?

The state decided to bury it near Afton, a community in Warren County itself. The area was one of the poorest in North Carolina, with a majority-black population. Promises made to the locals that the landfill would employ certain safety measures weren't taken seriously. Even the involvement of the EPA's Superfund program, which favored the site, made no one feel better. A January 1979 public hearing on the proposed landfill drew more than eight hundred protesters against the site.

WARREN COUNTY: FIGHTING ON MULTIPLE FRONTS

Soon, a collection of concerned citizens, civil rights activists, and lawyers filed a lawsuit against the landfill. Plans for its opening, however, remained unchanged. When the contaminated roadside dirt—enough for ten thousand truck-loads—was ready to be transported in the summer of 1982, nonviolent protesters were ready, too. Two hundred state troopers were deployed, and even the National Guard was put on alert.

The 1982 Warren County protests in North Carolina included civil disobedience, as demonstrated by these protesters, who locked arms to block a road to the contested landfill.

Notable among the protesters were Congressmen Walter E. Fauntroy and Ken Ferruccio, the
leader of a group formed years earlier—the Warren
County Citizens Concerned About PCB. Ferruccio
and his wife, Deborah, had just moved to the era,
and Ken was picked by his fellow group members
to be the leader for the effort. Hundreds of nonviolent protesters picketed the area where the PCB
trucks were parked, and blocked the roadways
to prevent them from mobilizing. Several hundred
arrests were made during a series of protests that
lasted six weeks. According to historian Ellen Grif-
fith Spears, the legendary civil rights activist and
head of the Southern Christian Leadership Conference (SCLC), Reverend Joseph Lowery, called
the proposed dumping "an assault on the life and
dignity of the citizens of Warren County." The cler-
gyman and his wife, Evelyn Lowery, were arrested
and spent a night in jail. Members of the National
Association for the Advancement of Colored People
(NAACP) also took part. Ken Ferruccio was himself
incarcerated and took the dramatic step of going
on a nineteen-day hunger strike while in prison.

In a 2014 editorial looking back on the protest,
Deborah Ferruccio explained that the protests did
not happen overnight, but were the result of longtime organization and four years worth of planning.
They were also part of a larger strategy to fight the
landfill. In the *Warren Record*, she wrote:

*[The] activist environmental justice move-
ment did not just happen as the PCB trucks
were rolling ... [Citizens] actively educated
themselves and the community on the
issues of landfill technology and the dangers of toxic waste. They spread the word
with old-fashioned telephone, door-to-door
and newspaper ad campaigns, with meetings in churches, civic halls and the county
courthouse. They hired an independent soil
scientist expert to evaluate the landfill site
and the state's plan. They built a scientific,
Constitutional and legal case against the
landfill, and they made this case at count-
less meetings, hearings and delegations to
the governor and his administration.*

The protests ultimately did not prevent the
landfill from happening, but the organization it
mobilized touched Warren County and echoed
the message across the nation that regular people were fighting back. Citizens were ready to
embrace environmentalism, especially when it
came to protecting communities, homes, and
schools. Efforts like the Warren County protests
would eventually lead to real government action,
including President William (Bill) J. Clinton approv-
ing an Office of Environmental Justice in 1994.

A MOVEMENT TRANSFORMS

In October 1991, a historic conference putting the environmental concerns of people of color at the forefront occurred in Washington, DC. It was the first meeting of the National People of Color Environmental Leadership Summit. African-American, Latino, Asian, Native American, and other activists gathered to promote their concerns, many of which they felt were overshadowed in the movement. They shared stories, including how all the residents of Reveilletown, Louisiana, an African-American town founded nearly one hundred years earlier, had been forced to relocate in 1989, because the nearby Georgia Gulf chemical plant had poisoned the town.

Summit delegates heard many discouraging and depressing tales of ecological crimes in people's own backyards, but were also inspired by tales of fighting back. These included first-hand accounts by activists from Arizona's Havasupai Nation who had stood up to uranium mining interests; Native Americans for a Clean Environment pushing to close nuclear-powered facilities in Oklahoma; and the Western Shoshone resisting nuclear testing on their ancestral territory in Nevada.

(continued on the next page)

(continued from the previous page)

Another topic of discussion was how environmental movements and organizations sometimes acted against the interests of communities of color because they did not consult these communities. One example noted at the summit was the schism between Ganados del Valle, a local rural development group in Los Ojos, New Mexico, and the Nature Conservancy. In 1975, the latter proposed that 22,000 acres (8094 hectares) in the area be designated to protect its natural beauty but had completely neglected to consult the local indigenous and Latino people, who for generations had practiced their own form of conservation on the land.

Western Shoshone Native American tribe members conduct a 2002 ceremony to protest the maintenance of a nuclear waste dump at Yucca Mountain in Nevada, a sacred site for them and other tribes.

THE HOLE IN THE OZONE, ACID RAIN, AND OTHER EMERGENCIES

A climate crisis that made big news in the 1980s was the growing hole in Earth's ozone layer. British physicist Joe Farman, alongside Brian Gardiner and Jon Shanklin, reported shocking news in the May 1985 issue of Nature, which became known as one of the most important environmental and scientific revelations of the century. Even scientists at the National Aeronautics and Space Administration (NASA) had overlooked what Farman and his team had discovered: levels in ozone, which formed a protective layer around the earth to prevent the overheating of the atmosphere, had fallen by as much as 40 percent from 1975 to 1984. Their discovery also affixed blame for this hole to chlorofluorocarbons (CFCs). CFCs were common in refrigeration technologies, and especially in spray-can aerosol products, like hair sprays and deodorants, and other consumer products, such as Styrofoam cups.

The campaign to ban CFCs soon jump-started a truly global effort. Even conservatives, traditionally hostile to regulation, like British Prime Minister Margaret Thatcher, agreed that action was needed, or humanity could suffer

dire consequences. People took action worldwide, from political leaders, to scientists, to high
school and college students. They started boy-
cotts against product made with CFCs, and the
businesses that produced them. By September
1987, the anti-CFC effort was so mainstream
that an international coalition of nations signed
a CFC ban, to go into effect on January 1, 1989.
This agreement, called the Montreal Protocol,
has gone through many revisions over the years,
and is still valid. It is considered one of, if not
the most, successful environmental treaties ever.
This is because scientists have reported that the
ozone layers have somewhat recovered, and the
ozone itself will return to its pre-1980 levels in
several decades, if CFCs continue to be banned.

Another pervasive problem has been acid rain.
Rain that is acidic below a certain level occurs
when emissions of sulfur dioxide and nitrogen
oxides pollute the air. Acid rain weakens trees,
depletes nutrients in soils, and releases alumi-
num and other potentially toxic substances. It also
corrodes limestone and marble and can adversely
affect wildlife where acidity is at its highest. By
the 1970s and especially the 1980s, the problem
became a household name, affecting large parts
of North America, Europe, and other continents.
The problem has lessened in the last two decades
due to a delayed reaction from the effects of the

Acid rain was responsible for the destruction of this spruce forest in the Jizera Mountains of the Czech Republic.

Clean Air Act of 1970 and other laws, including those that were rolled out in the late 1980s and early 1990s.

The acid rain and ozone hole issues affected local communities, as well as the global population. The focus of a worldwide effort to protect the environment soon shifted to problems that were little understood at first, but eventually took center stage: global warming and catastrophic climate change.

EARTH DAY, 1990: A NEW GENERATION

A new generation of activists, especially youth, was inspired in 1990 by a reboot, so to speak, of Earth Day, the 1970 environmentalism event. At the request of a group of other movement leaders, Denis Hayes returned to organize the event again. This time, according to the official Earth Day site, the events of April 22, 1990, ended up "mobilizing 200 million people in 141 countries and lifting environmental issues onto the world stage." A massive concert in Central Park, along with a two-hour television special that aired on the ABC network, focused world attention on both the challenges the world was facing as the twenty-first century loomed, and what could be done to meet them.

THE IPCC, EARTH SUMMIT, AND KYOTO

By the late 1980s and early 1990s, environmental concerns and activism had become mainstream. This was true even in the United States, where consumerism and some hostility to government regulation still divided public sectors. Around the world, citizens in many nations took the various crises facing the planet even more seriously. In 1988, the United Nations (UN) established the Intergovernmental Panel on Climate Change (IPCC) in Switzerland, which combined the efforts of the UN's Environment Programme (UNEP) and the World Meteorological Organization (WMO). The IPCC's members combined and analyzed reports from hundreds of international climate scientists, politicians and policymakers, in order to get a full picture of whether climate change was happening, and what could be done about it.

The twentieth anniversary of Earth Day in 1990, the IPCC's works, and other smaller-scale environmental campaigns, were a prologue to the 1992 United Nations Conference on Environment and Development (UNCED), also known as the Earth Summit. It was the biggest meeting of world leaders ever convened, and aimed to come up with ideas on how to continue economic development and sync it with environmental protection. One of the major divisions was what commitments would be required of poorer, developing nations, who needed jobs, opportunity, and environmental regulations, versus those required of the richest, most industrially developed nations.

Leaders of the Global South (poorer, still developing nations) asked that countries like the United States and those in the European Union use

A panel from the United Nations Conference on Environment and Development that took place in June 1992 in Rio de Janeiro, Brazil, is shown here.

their vast wealth to help subsidize development. Their monies could help build opportunity for those in Africa, South America, and Asia, while maintaining high standards of environmental protection. It was only fair, they argued, because the United States and other leading economies were by far the worst polluters, with populations creating far more greenhouse gases than populations in the Global South. Ultimately, the United Nations Framework Convention on Climate Change (UNFCCC) was ratified at the conference. The framework set nonbinding, or voluntary, limits on greenhouse gas emissions.

Finally, a 1997 meeting in Kyoto, Japan, marked a concrete effort by many nations to reduce greenhouse gas emissions contributing to global warming. The agreement they came up with was the Kyoto Protocol, which called for reducing six greenhouse gases to levels about 5.2 percent below what they had been in 1990. Large, periodic add-ons to Kyoto and other international efforts occur almost every year.

CHAPTER FOUR

THE STAKES GET HIGHER

As a movement, environmentalism has certainly had many successes. The world itself would be a far worse place had it not been for the hard work of the many people and groups who have been part of it. Nevertheless, trying to alleviate the harms that human neglect has caused on our planet can often feel like a losing game. In the modern era, activists on many fronts have differed greatly about what approaches work best, and which ones are appropriate for different situations. Under what circumstances should environmentalists work closely with government, industry, and other profit-driven interests? When should they push them harder, or opt out of such alliances?

A COLLABORATIVE APPROACH

Many groups have done a great deal of good, especially in the conservation of wilderness areas and

An old barn shows its wear and tear from use and the weather. Acid rain and other phenomena can wreak havoc on both natural and manmade things.

nature preserves. They work closely with other parties to buy or lease territory, maintain ecosystems, and protect sensitive areas. Other groups take on pollution by teaming up with companies that want to make their operations more environmentally friendly, or "green." Such efforts might even be combined in a three-way partnership: a nonprofit environmental group, a business or industry group, and a relevant EPA branch or state office of environmental protection. There are also cases in which a manufacturer might get city tax breaks if they adhere to standards that limit pollutions in their immediate neighborhood. Or, a green nonprofit could work closely with a private real estate developer to maximize their energy systems, floor plans, and grounds, and to use the least amount of energy resources.

For private companies, working with environmental organizations might be multipronged. They may need positive public relations and the reputation-building effects of taking on such endeavors. Others may recognize that behaving responsibly, despite high up-front costs, will save them money in the long run. Still others may do it because the company's leadership sincerely believes in promoting environmentalist goals.

THE ADVERSARIAL APPROACH

Other activists, scholars of the movement, and journalists covering the issues point out that many communities and activists are dissatisfied with the pace of change, especially the kind of change that occurs from collaboration, voluntary measures, and other "soft" types of persuasion and influence. Many believe that the largest environmental groups—collectively known as "Big Green" or the "Big 10"—need to become more aggressive.

Others believe that grassroots activists need to put the pressure on locally and nationally with actions that get news coverage, shaming noncompliant parties into improved antipollution efforts and policy changes.

More radical voices point out that mainstream groups sometimes avoid direct action that could draw criticism from the government, corporations, and the public at large, including big and small donors that companies depend on. Notable donors might even include energy, fossil-fuel, real estate, and other companies that might not appreciate it if environmental legislation or campaigns go too far, or hurt their profitability.

Smaller, less mainstream environmental activist efforts take a more adversarial approach. They treat coal companies, unsympathetic governments, and others they feel are dragging down the effort to protect the earth as adversaries, rather than friends—respectfully and legally. Many of these less mainstream environmental groups work in the tradition of environmental justice. To them, for instance, a crisis like climate change is an ongoing emergency that will leave us with a dangerous and unequal world. It would be a place where richer people and nations are better protected from extreme weather, flooding, and other likely consequences, while the poor and powerless suffer from extremes. In other situations, local

BILL MCKIBBEN: CLIMATE CHANGE WARRIOR

For nearly three decades, writer and journalist Bill McKibben has been one of the world's most visible and active environmentalists. He uses writing and protesting to boost awareness about climate change, pointing out what a dire emergency humanity is facing. The election of Ronald Reagan to the presidency—along with Reagan and many Republicans' perceived hostility to environmental protections—convinced the young McKibben, then attending Harvard University, to dedicate his life to environmentalism.

McKibben published his first book, *The End of Nature*, in 1989. It was, as his website notes, was the "first book for a general audience about climate change." McKibben felt that climate change was not solvable via conventional means and minor fixes, but by large masses of people changing their world views, lifestyles, and consumption choices, and pushing the government for radical change.

By the late 2000s, McKibben, like many others, had grown impatient and frustrated with the slow and often indifferent response of government to climate change. He then cofounded 350 .org, named after the 350 parts per million that many scientists believe is the upper safe limit for

(continued on the next page)

(continued from the previous page)

carbon dioxide in Earth's atmosphere. The group has dedicated its resources to change all levels of government and to organize protests. One of 350.org's most visible campaigns has been the effort to block the construction of the Keystone XL, a major oil pipeline moving Canadian oil to the United States. Among its most innovative and effective tactics has been its divestment campaigns. They encouraged students at hundreds of colleges and universities, as well as many cities and states, to pressure institutions to remove their financial investments in oil companies and other enterprises that profit from fossil fuels.

Students call upon President Barack Obama to reject further building of the Keystone XL pipeline during this protest across from the White House in March 2014.

groups engage in acts of civil disobedience—often risking their bodies and safety—to slow or shut down things they feel are a threat to their environment.

RESTRAINED OR RADICAL?

While some criticize mainstream environmentalism for being too cozy with corporations, an accompanying complaint is that large parts of the movement have not changed with the times. Their out-of-touch ways lessen the impact, and governmental partnerships, which made sense in the 1960s and 1970s, produce diminishing returns. Preserving pockets of wilderness and beautiful places for some people to enjoy (mostly those with resources), while the rest of the world slowly becomes uninhabitable, has been likened to renovating one's living room while the rest of the house is on fire.

Consequently, radical environmentalists believe that more aggressive, direct actions are needed to achieve immediate, concrete goals, such as blocking a fracking operation in a small town. They also work to inspire others to join the cause, to influence the media to report on polluters, and to publicize the sometimes harsh blowback experienced by activists from companies and law enforcement.

Most of the environmental movement adheres to a philosophy of nonviolence, with many activists incorporating civil disobedience into their advocacy. Some activists break laws by participating in sit-ins, die-ins, or other such actions, which puts them at risk for being arrested or manhandled by police officers. Even so, they generally do not hit or attack others, and avoid damaging property. But every group embraces different tactics, and there are those who believe that property damage and more aggressive efforts are acceptable.

EARTH FIRST! AND ELF

Two groups took extreme measures to fight environmental destruction: Earth First! and the Earth Liberation Front. Earth First!

A police investigator looks over the burnt remains of hotel buildings in Vail, Colorado, a 1998 instance of arson later blamed on radical environmentalists from the Earth Liberation Front (ELF).

formed in 1980 as a radical alternative to mainstream organizations. Its slogan "No Compromise in Defense of Mother Earth!" and its loose, decentralized structure encouraged direct action that was sometimes confrontational. Without national or international leaders to answer to, members of the group often occupied logging operations and building sites. Group members sabotaged equipment, and booby-trapped trees with spikes to prevent cutting. They also blocked logging crews from worksites by standing or lying down in front of bulldozers and other construction vehicles.

The Earth Liberation Front (ELF) is a splinter group from Earth First! It is even more radical and works both secretly and openly, frequently breaking the law. For example, ELF set fire to a ski resort in Vail, Colorado, in 1998, and committed other acts of sabotage and arson. While some of their allies in the mainstream movement understand their motivations, most environmentalists have criticized ELF's tactics as being counterproductive. They say ELF harms the cause more than helps it, needlessly endangering and inconveniencing others.

The Federal Bureau of Investigation (FBI) and others have investigated ELF and have labeled their actions ecoterrorism. Meanwhile, a founder of Earth First! and self-declared "eco-warrior" David Foreman, explained his motives in getting involved with often illegal, but nonviolent (at least when it came to humans), tactics to *People* magazine in 1990. After he was arrested, Foreman declared:

> *When we damage a bulldozer, or chain ourselves to one to protest the building of a road through a wilderness area, we feel like the abolitionists who helped slaves escape from the South through the Underground Railroad. We're breaking the law for a higher ethical ideal.*

STANDING ROCK: BODIES ON THE LINE

One notable example of direct action in the face of seemingly overwhelming odds was the massive protest against the Dakota Access Pipeline. Begun by activists of the Standing Rock Sioux tribe, the action was supported by a wide array of legal and environmental groups, including many indigenous ones. The protest was heavily publicized with #NODAPL on social media sites like Twitter.

Standing Rock protesters summoned hundreds of supporters to their camp in North Dakota beginning around April 2016. They insisted that the pipeline threatened the local environment and would run too close to the tribe's water supplies and ancient burial grounds. These "water protectors," as they became known, waged a month-long campaign. They blocked trucks and other vehicles working on the project, as well as occupied areas where pipeline employees were already working. Financial support came in from around the world, helping those who were willing to put their bodies on the line on the ground. A makeshift tent community developed in the area, and it grew into a small city, which served as the headquarters for those who pitched in with the protest efforts.

The #NODAPL activists faced aggressive and often brutal treatment from pipeline employees, private security contractors, and law enforcement from regional and out-of-state agencies. Without warning, encampments were violently cleared out, and rubber bullets and water cannons were fired on the activists, even in freezing temperatures. Luckily, no one on either side of the argument was killed, but the number of injuries was in the hundreds for the nonviolent activists. Mass arrests were made and for those who were imprisoned, many reported that they faced cruel treatment. Still others were followed, watched, and harassed by police and pipeline employees. After months of pressure, the administration of President Barack Obama seemed ready to work on rerouting the pipeline in order to avoid the indigenous lands. However, the 2016 election of President Donald J. Trump reversed the efforts. Trump rescinded all Obama-era measures, and oil began flowing near Standing Rock in spring 2018.

A DANGEROUS OCCUPATION

As a passion, hobby, or even full-time job, being an environmental advocate in places like the United States and Canada is a relatively safe vocation. However, hundreds of environmental activists all over the world have given their lives for their cause. Many more are injured, pressured, or otherwise intimidated from standing their ground. The *Guardian* reported in February 2018 that "almost four people a week were killed worldwide in struggles against mines, plantations, poachers, and infrastructure projects," with a death toll of 187 in 2017 alone. Activists work in dangerous locales, often among populations suffering massive inequality. Too frequently, minority indigenous activists are persecuted by private interests and their own police forces and governments.

Few stories have captured the world's attention like that of Berta Cáceres, a Nicaraguan activist of the indigenous Lenca people. Since 1993,

(continued on the next page)

(continued from the previous page)

Cáceres fought against illegal logging and policies harmful to her people's homeland. In 2013, she organized a blockade to prevent a Honduran company, Desarrollos Energéticos SA (DESA), from building a dam. For a whole year, they were successful in blocking the project, despite heavy pushback from private security forces and the Honduran military. Later, a foreign partner of DESA pulled out, and the dam project was cancelled, with activists declaring victory.

However, it was a bittersweet triumph. A community leader named Tomas Garcia was killed earlier, with others detained and even tortured or attacked with machetes. Cáceres had endured death threats for years, but they increased in the wake of the DESA showdown. Gunmen killed Cáceres in her home on March 3, 2016. Just twelve days later, a colleague named Nelson Garcia was also murdered. The killings shocked the world. If they hoped to extinguish the passion of the nation's activists, the brutality of the assailants surely accomplished the exact opposite.

ACTION AROUND THE WORLD

In May 2016, more than a thousand anticoal activists took to kayaks and boats to stage a water

This May 2016 floating protest in the port of Newcastle in Australia blocked coal ships as part of an action demanding a move away from using fossil fuels.

blockade on the harbor of Newcastle, the site of the largest coal-exporting operation in Australia. With this symbolic action, they demanded that the Australian government take action to ease their nation off of fossil fuels, and concentrate on renewables. At least sixty-six protesters were arrested. The blockade, organized by umbrella group Break Free from Fossil Fuels, became an annual event.

On the other side of the world, the New York City–based West Harlem Environmental Action,

Inc. (WE ACT) has done its share to promote policies and laws that address climate change and environmental racism in upper Manhattan. Founded in 1988 by Peggy Shepard, Chuck Sutton, and Vernice Miller-Travis to oppose the building of a sewage treatment plant and the siting of another bus depot in the Harlem area, WE ACT's actions over time have helped push successful legislation at the city, state, and federal levels. One such effort was a march of five thousand people in October 2017 to commemorate the five-year anniversary of Hurricane Sandy on the city.

Organized under the #Sandy5 hashtag, WE ACT brought together storm survivors from Puerto Rico's devastating Hurricane Maria in September 2017, others who braved the Irma and Katrina weather events, and Hurricane Sandy survivors demanding immediate and real action by the government to address climate change issues. WE ACT member Nasib McIntosh wrote the following in a blog post on the group's website regarding what motivates him, fellow activists, and concerned community members:

> [T]he promises made by our elected officials are still unfulfilled. As rampant inequality continues to define New York City's social landscape, climate change threatens to aggravate and increase these

deeply rooted disparities. Across the city, plans to build protection along the coastlines of highly vulnerable Hurricane Evacuation Zones are either underwhelming or still in development ... low-income and black and brown communities—already contending with lack of access to social services and environmental discrimination— can expect to deal with what trends confirm are more frequent and devastating extreme weather events.

Wangari Maathai, the Kenyan founder of the Green Belt sustainability movement, and known especially for tying environmentalism to women's rights and issues, received a Nobel Prize in 2004.

Based in Nairobi, Kenya, the Green Belt Movement (GBM) is a grassroots nonprofit that empowers women to fight deforestation by planting trees, preserving water in the face of climate change, and promoting sustainable livelihoods and independent communities. It has creatively tied environmentalism with community engagement and women's rights, inspiring many movements worldwide to emulate it. GBM was founded in 1977 by Wangari Maathai. Maathai, a Kenyan biologist, politician, and longtime activist, was one of the first women in her region of Africa to earn a doctorate degree. Issues like land use, forestry, agriculture, and conflict over resources, especially for indigenous communities worldwide that still depend on the land for the livelihoods, make GBM and organizations like it an important part of and inspiration for the environmental movement as a whole.

CHAPTER FIVE

TAKING ACTION: WHAT YOU CAN DO

W hether you plan to one day pursue environmental activism as a livelihood, or merely want to pitch in your free time to make a difference, there are dozens of paths you can take. They depend on what you are comfortable with doing, your strengths and passions, where you live, and how extensive you want your involvement to be.

FINDING YOUR CAUSE

What issue really motivates you to get involved? Some are concerned about global warming, climate change, and extreme weather, and want to force industry and government to cut down on greenhouse gases. Others want to promote renewable energy sources, like wind, solar, and hydropower. Another subset of activists may work against soil depletion, or oppose factory farming and other activities that use too many of our resources. Still others bring it back to local concerns, like protesting a new incinerator or landfill in their neighborhood, or activities such as fracking, or waging campaigns to improve conditions in their areas. On whatever front someone opts to help out, there is likely an organization working on that same issue somewhere nearby.

START YOUR OWN ORGANIZATION

There may not be a group that you can join locally (or remotely) that addresses a environmental issue that is important to you or specific to your community. Why not start your own, then? Melati and Isabel Wijsen, two sisters from the island nation of Bali, were concerned about one of their nation's most pressing ecological issues. According to CNN, Bali was practically drowning in plastic bags (they are second to China when it comes to plastic pollution). The Wijsen sisters were inspired by the annual "trash season" that now dumps piles of mostly plastic trash on their nation's beaches annually, and decided to do something about it. Incredibly, they were just ten and twelve years old when they began their journey.

"There's no escaping it here," Melati Wijsen told CNN. "The plastic problem is so in your face, and we thought: 'Well, who's going to do something about it?'" Learning about movement leaders like Martin

Sister activists Melati (*left*) and Isabel Wijsen (*right*) hold their Bambi Award during the November 2017 ceremony in Berlin, Germany. They won in the Award for Our Earth category.

Luther King Jr. and Nelson Mandela, the sisters sprang into action in 2013. They started their own environmental group, Bye Bye Plastic Bags, and set out to persuade their government to ban plastic bags entirely. Melati told Indonesia Expat, "We decided we did not want to wait until we got diplomas and went to university. We thought right now is the time to do something, as kids. We studied all the issues Bali is facing and chose garbage because that is what most impacted our daily lives."

It helped to have connections at their environmentally oriented Green School. A teacher invited them to the Global Issues Network conference in their hometown, and soon the Wijsen sisters were also visiting other schools in their area. Spreading their message helped them to become speakers in the prestigious TED Talks lecture series, and guest speakers at the United Nations. More importantly, a petition they started gained more than one hundred thousand signatures. They even waged a hunger strike (as CNN indicated, with the help of a dietician) to get Bali's governor to eventually sign a memorandum that will hopefully become official

VANDANA SHIVA: ENVIRONMENTALISM AND FOOD SOVEREIGNTY

One of the most prominent activists that ties her environmentalism to concrete, social-justice goals is physicist and activist Vandana Shiva. Upon returning home to India after continuing her studies in Canada, Shiva discovered that a forest she enjoyed as a child had been cut down, and a stream had been drained to make way for an apple orchard. This sparked her initial interest in environmental issues.

She founded the Research Foundation for Science, Technology, and Natural Resource Policy (RFSTN) in 1982. While fighting against logging operations and dam construction in her native India, she also gained prominence for criticizing the use of artificial pesticides and fertilizers in agriculture as part of the Green Revolution. The Green Revolution aimed to significantly increase food production in places like India. It also depended on vast amounts of land being used for a single crop, and later on genetically modified organisms (GMOs), which Shiva warned, could threaten the food supply. She also opposed the loss of biodiversity that GMOs cause, and the new costs that these food production techniques require. Shiva maintained that the results of these activities were driving more farmers into poverty.

In response, RFSTN has fought GMO promoters—such as corporations like Monsanto—by promoting alternatives to farmers and governments, and establishing dozens of seed banks to preserve local and unique strains of food crops and other plant life. She has tied environmental protection and the defense of farmers together to an anti-corporate model that many communities and groups around the world, especially indigenous activist organizations, have emulated and adapted for their own struggles.

and ban most or all bag production in Bali in 2018.

YOU CAN DO IT, TOO

You don't need connections, television appearances, or financial support like the Wijsen sisters to do something bold and creative for the environment. All you need is your passion, and ways to connect to others who share your goals. Climate change action might be your specialty, or simply organizing a group to help clean up and restore some parkland or wilderness in your area. You can research

Every little bit counts when it comes to helping the earth, including simply volunteering with friends or fellow students to clean a local park.

what the biggest polluter in your area is, and figure out what steps to take to encourage or press them to change their ways. Another way of helping is to volunteer for an established environmental group, such as the Sierra Club, World Wildlife Fund (WWF), Greenpeace, the Nature Conservancy, and others.

The National Wildlife Federation (NWF) provides some steps to start an environmental group in your school or neighborhood. If you are starting completely from scratch, below are some recommendations from NWF:

1. Do your homework. Are there at least five or six other people (students, neighbors, etc.) who share your desire to form a group? Can you think of other groups in your community who might mentor your group or give advice? What about other youth groups that might support your messages or goals?
2. Get and confirm adult sponsors. If it is a school club, a sponsor will usually be a teacher or other staff member.
3. Schedule an interest session. Publicize a meeting somewhere, whether it is at a park, the public library, a classroom, or other space at your school. Ask yourselves, why are we here and what do we hope to accomplish.
4. Have your first meeting. Advertise the first

meeting of your environmental club with flyers, posters, and other materials. Alert a local paper about your meeting, because many are small and local enough to actually cover it. Spread the word via social networks, including Twitter, Instagram, and Facebook.

For the full list of tips and suggestion, visit the NWF's website (nwf.org), which also has tips on how to "green your school" via one of the largest programs of its kind.

BRUSH UP AND PREPARE

There are many classes you can take if you are interested in activism. If you want to help tackle climate issues, endangered species, or similar issues, some more ambitious professions to consider include becoming a scientist. Concentrating in biology, geology, chemistry, physics, atmospheric science, meteorology, and many other fields will equip you to explore and write about environmental issues. Environmental science is its own interdisciplinary academic field, and has become quite popular. To get involved, you will want to take as many STEM (science, technology, engineering, and math) courses as possible.

Law is another field that has attracted the ecologically minded. Many organizations use lawyers to help draft legislation, challenge government decisions, and work with organization members to beat back legal challenges and prosecution. While it can generally be a lucrative career, few environmental lawyers get into the field for financial gain. Many work for nonprofits and governments at all levels, and earn decent but unspectacular salaries. History, English, and similar humanities classes are good for aspiring legal students.

Another route to making a difference is via journalism and writing. There is always a demand for citizen journalists, alternative journalists, and mainstream ones to cover the environmental beat. One way to break into the industry is to start an environmental newsletter for your school or to join your school paper or yearbook committee. You can cover relevant issues via a blog or Tumblr account, or any medium you can imagine. Remember to always cite copyrighted content from quoted sources, and to always vet and confirm any news or information you post to make sure it is true. Avoid defaming or doxxing anyone—that is, revealing their identities, personal information, or anything else that could make them vulnerable to scrutiny by authorities or unsavory types online.

STAYING SAFE, ONLINE AND OFF

Whether you blog about your club's upcoming participation in Earth Day, or connect with fellow young environmentalists via Twitter, remember to take steps to ensure your safety and that of your fellow group members. If you are meeting someone who wants to join your group for the first time, make sure they can prove who they say they are. Use caution when meeting them, and opt for a busy, public place, such as a library or coffee shop.

When it comes to taking specific actions, it is good to get advice from trusted adults about the right thing to do before jumping into anything. Consult parents, family members, or mentors such as teachers, guidance counselors, or faith leaders. Nowadays, students participating in various movements can often be found at marches, rallies, and protests. Still, anyone below the age of eighteen is considered a minor, and it is essential for any group that accepts the help of minors to get proper consent forms signed by adults, when necessary.

In addition, adults can be held liable for actions by underage associates. It is extremely risky and wrongheaded for someone in a position of authority to abuse the trust of youth in their care (or that of their parents and fellow educators). This is especially true if they encourage them to do anything dangerous, unethical, or illegal. If you feel stuck in any situation where someone—adult or peer—is pressing you to do something you do not feel comfortable with, even if it seems harmless, leave the situation and report your concerns to another trusted adult.

THE ACTIVIST AS CONSUMER

Some people believe that consumer choices can help push corporations and others to make products that are less harmful to the earth. To some extent, this has helped. Examples include activists who motivate auto manufacturers to build hybrid and electric cars, and press architects, engineers, and urban planners to construct "green buildings" that use better design as well as solar and wind technologies to power them.

On the other hand, there are better ways of creating less waste. These include cutting down on the need for landfills and on the wasteful and polluting manufacturing processes that make products we want (but don't necessarily need) for our comfort and well-being. There are some minor fixes individuals can make to extend the life of things they own, and to downplay consumerism in their own lives:

- Make do with older models of computers, televisions, and smartphones, as opposed

This Toyota Prius Plug-In Hybrid vehicle, part of a new wave of sustainable automobiles, was on display at the North American International Auto Show in Detroit, Michigan, in January 2010.

to always investing in newer ones every one or two years.

- Avoid fast food, which uses excess packaging and is often produced in ways that are harmful to animals and the environment.
- Pass on consumer products that use too much packaging or buy used products online or from friends.
- Use recyclables whenever possible, such as reusable bags when doing your shopping.

- Carefully plan your shopping trips to avoid buying excess food or other products that may spoil if you do not end up eating or using them.
- Minimize water consumption. Do not let water run while you are not using it. Low-flow shower heads and toilets are great ideas, if you can convince family members to install them.
- Use less detergents and other cleansers when doing laundry, and wash full loads versus half-empty ones.
- Reduce electric use. Turn off lights in rooms that are not in use. Turn off and unplug electrical appliances, computers, televisions, and other consumer items that suck up juice even when they are off.
- Convince your family to lower the thermostat during cooler days and raise it on warmer ones.

"ARE WE DOING ENOUGH?"

Many impassioned environmentalists often ask whether they are doing all they can to preserve Earth and protect it for the future. They also wonder, "Are our tactics working?" The answers, depending on how one looks at them, can be encouraging in some ways. Take Greenpeace as an example. It has had tremendous successes since the 1970s, including victories in getting many forms of commercial whaling banned, pressuring governments to give up nuclear testing, and protecting wild swathes of wilderness everywhere.

On the other hand, the news can be discouraging and downright frightening. Environmental writer and lawyer James Gustave Speth, writing in 2008 for Yale Environment 360, was not optimistic. He gloomily declared:

> Half the world's tropical and temperate forests are now gone. [D]eforestation in the tropics continues at about an acre a second, and has for decades. Half the planet's wetlands are gone. An estimated 90 percent of the large predator fish are gone, and 75 percent of marine fisheries are now overfished or fished to capacity. Almost half of the corals are gone or are seriously threatened. Species are disappearing at rates about 1,000 times faster than normal. The planet has not seen such a spasm of extinction in 65 million years, since the dinosaurs disappeared. Desertification claims a Nebraska-sized area of productive capacity each year globally. Persistent toxic chemicals can now be found by the dozens in essentially each and every one of us.

An overhead view of this patch of Amazon rain forest highlights the deforestation that humans directly cause there and in many other places around the world.

These scary figures can make anyone want to give up. Or, they could be dire enough to inspire a newer and bolder generation to take more dramatic actions. These actions aren't limited to laws and new ways of saving energy and recycling, but include a massive reordering of how business, farming, and society at large work at the deepest levels to avert a coming catastrophe late in the twenty-first century, when the world may cease to be habitable for human beings.

TIMELINE

1892 John Muir founds the Sierra Club.

1896 The Massachusetts Audubon Society is formed.

1905 US president Theodore Roosevelt forms the Bureau of Forestry.

1951 The Nature Conservancy is founded.

1962 Rachel Carson publishes her landmark book, *Silent Spring.*

1963 The original Clean Air Act is passed by the US Congress and signed by US president Lyndon B. Johnson.

1964 The Wilderness Act is signed into law.

1969 The Santa Barbara Oil Spill pollutes the Pacific Ocean, galvanizing the environmental movement.

1970 The First Earth Day event is held with nationwide participation.

US president Richard Nixon forms the Environmental Protection Agency (EPA).

1971 Greenpeace is founded, originally to protest nuclear proliferation and testing.

1972 Dichlorodiphenyltrichloroethane (DDT) is banned in the United States.

1973 Congress passes the Endangered Species Act, which is signed into law by President Nixon.

1978 The Love Canal toxic disaster in New York State refocuses public attention on the environment.

1985 A team of scientists publishes their discovery of a hole in the ozone layer caused by human activity in Nature journal.

1987 The Montreal Protocol is signed by the United States, Japan, Canada, and other nations, banning the use of CFCs.

1988 The United Nations' Intergovernmental Panel on Climate Change (IPCC) is set up.

1992 The United Nations Framework Convention on Climate Change (UNFCCC) requests voluntary cuts in greenhouse gases from member nations.

1997 UNFCCC member nations sign the Kyoto Protocol, establishing targets of how much of six greenhouse gases to reduce to pre-1990 levels.

2005 Hurricane Katrina becomes one of the deadliest and most destructive hurricanes to ever hit the United States, killing more than 1,800 and causing much of New Orleans, Louisiana, to flood.

2007 China overtakes the United States as the greatest emitter of greenhouse gases.

2016–2017 The Dakota Access Pipeline protests, headed by the Standing Rock Sioux Tribe, attract worldwide attention.

GLOSSARY

carcinogen A substance known or suspected to noticeably increase the chances of cancer for those exposed to it.

civil disobedience A form of peaceful political protest that involves refusal to comply with laws, orders, or fines that one considers illegitimate.

conservation A subset of the environmental movement that concentrates on preserving, protecting, or restoring part of the natural environment.

counterculture Cultural values and behaviors that run contrary to those of an established society.

deep ecology A philosophy and movement that considers all living things equally important, with humans only a component of the big picture.

die-in A theatrical protest in which activists simulate dying.

divestment To sell or deprive another from an asset for financial, political, or social gain.

eco-terrorism Radical and often illegal actions, including sabotage and arson.

environmental racism Refers to the injustices that communities of color often face when it comes to being overexposed to pollutants, polluting facilities, landfills, and other toxic hazards, versus those of richer and whiter communities.

forestry The science and study of taking care of woodland areas.

fracking A highly controversial resource extraction technique used for oil, natural gas, and other fuels, in which high-pressure liquids are injected into the ground to free up these substances for removal.

galvanize To shock or surprise people into taking action.

grassroots Describes the activism of ordinary people at the ground level of a movement.

greenhouse gas A gas released into Earth's atmosphere that contributes to climate change by absorbing the sun's radiation, such as carbon dioxide.

imperiled To put in danger of injury or destruction.

incinerator A furnace or machine that burns waste and garbage.

occupational disease An illness one develops because of conditions on the job.

prologue An event or development that serves as an introduction.

renewables Refers to forms of energy that are not depleted, including wind and solar power, unlike fossil fuels.

status quo A current situation that should remain, or is perceived to stay, the same.

Superfund A government program that distributes money to people and communities affected by environmental disasters.

swathes Long rows of cut grass or grains.

teach-in A lecture or talk, usually given informally, about an important current issue.

FOR MORE INFORMATION

Earthroots
401 Richmond Street West, Suite 410
Toronto, ON M5V 3A8
Canada
(416) 599-0152
Email: info@earthroots.org
Website: https://earthroots.org
Facebook: @Earthroots.Coalition
Twitter: @Earthroots
Earthroots is a grassroots environmental organi-
zation using research, education, and direct
action to preserve the wildlife, wilderness, and
watersheds of Ontario.

Environmental Defense Fund (EDF)
1875 Connecticut Avenue NW, Suite 600
Washington, DC 20009
(800) 684-3322
Email: members@edf.org
Website: https://www.edf.org
Facebook and Twitter: @EnvDefenseFund
Founded in 1967, the Environmental Defense Fund
is a major environmental nonprofit based in the
Untied States that boasts two million members
and a staff of more than seven hundred policy
experts, economists, and scientists.

Green Communities Canada
416 Chambers Street, 2nd Floor

Peterborough, ON K9H 3V1
Canada
(705) 745-7479
Email: info@greencommunitiescanada.org
Website: http://greencommunitiescanada.org
Facebook: @Green.Communities.Canada1
Twitter: @GCCCanada
Green Communities Canada is a national consortium
of community organizations in Canada encourag-
ing green technologies, conservation, and other
environmentally minded programs and actions.

Greenpeace
702 H Street NW, Suite 300
Washington, DC 20001
(800) 722-6995
Email: info@wdc.greenpeace.org
Website: https://www.greenpeace.org/usa
Facebook, Instagram, and Twitter:
@greenpeaceusa
YouTube: Greenpeace USA
Greenpeace is an independent nonprofit that uses
a multipronged strategy, including nonviolent
direct action, and is one of the most prolific,
well funded, and succcssful environmental
groups in the world.

Sierra Club
2101 Webster Street, Suite 1300

Oakland, CA 94612
(415) 977-5500
Email: information@sierraclub.org
Website: https://www.sierraclub.org
Facebook and Twitter: @SierraClub
Instagram: @sierraclub
YouTube: NationalSierraClub
The Sierra Club is one of the oldest and most influential environmental organizations in the world, with more than three million members and supporters.

United States Environmental Protection Agency (EPA)
1200 Pennsylvania Avenue, NW
Washington, DC 20460
Website: https://www.epa.gov
Facebook and Twitter: @EPA
Instagram: @epagov
YouTube: U.S. Environmental Protection Agency
The United States Environmental Protection Agency (EPA) is the nation's federal government agency dedicated to protecting the natural environment and employs more than fifteen thousand full-time scientists, engineers, lawyers, and other specialists.

WE ACT for Environmental Justice
1854 Amsterdam Avenue, 2nd Floor
New York, NY 10031

(212) 961-1000
Email: info@weact.org
Website: https://www.weact.org
Facebook: @weactforej
Instagram and Twitter: @weact4ej
YouTube: WE ACT for Environmental Justice
WE ACT is a community-based, grassroots envi-
ronmental organization that has fought for
cleaner air and against environmental racism
since its inception in 1988.

FOR FURTHER READING

Appleby, Alex. *Happy Earth Day!* New York, NY: Gareth Stevens Publishing, 2014.

Archer, Jules. *To Save the Earth: The American Environmental Movement.* New York, NY: Sky Pony Press, 2016.

Braun, Eric. *Taking Action to Help the Environment.* Minneapolis, MN: Lerner Publications, 2017.

Cunningham, Anne C. *Environmental Racism and Classism.* New York, NY: Greenhaven Publishing, 2017.

Heos, Bridget. *It's Getting Hot in Here: The Past, the Present, and the Future of Global Warming.* Boston, MA: Houghton Mifflin Harcourt, 2015.

Kopp, Megan. *Living in a Sustainable Way: Green Communities.* St. Catharines, Ontario: Crabtree Publishing Company, 2016.

Lebrecque, Ellen. *Drilling and Fracking.* Ann Arbor, MI: Cherry Lake Publishing, 2018.

Naughton, Diane. *Our Green Future.* New York, NY: Cambridge University Press, 2014.

Rauf, Don. *Protecting the Environment Through Service Learning.* New York, NY: Rosen Publishing, Inc., 2015.

Simons, Rae. *How Does the Environment Affect You?* Vestal, NY: Village Earth Press, 2014.

Steoff, Rebecca. *The Environmental Movement: Then and Now.* North Mankato, MN: Capstone Press, 2018.

BIBLIOGRAPHY

Ahmed, Amal. "We Can't Truly Protect the Environment Unless We Tackles Social Justice Issues, Too." *Popular Science*, February 26, 2018. https://www.popsci.com/environmentalism -inclusive-justice.

Beck, Eckardt C. "The Love Canal Tragedy." EPA Journal, January 1979. https://archive.epa.gov /epa/aboutepa/love-canal-tragedy.html.

Biello, David. "Where Did the Carter White House's Solar Panels Go?" *Scientific American*, August 6, 2010. https://www.scientificamerican.com /article/carter-white-house-solar-panel-array.

Childs, Martin. "Joe Farman: Scientist Who First Uncovered the Hole in the Ozone Layer." *Independent*, May 20, 2013. https://www .independent.co.uk/news/obituaries /joe-farman-scientist-who-first-uncovered -the-hole-in-the-ozone-layer-8624438.html.

Davis, Karen. "From Bali to the World's Stage; Meet Melati and Isabel Wijsen." Indonesia Expat, July 26, 2016. http://indonesiaexpat.biz /meet-the-expats/from-bali-to-the-worlds-stage -meet-melati-and-isabel-wijsen.

D'Costa, Krystal. "Tracing the Trickle-Down in Roman Recycling." *Scientific American* blog, October 3, 2011. https://blogs .scientificamerican.com/anthropology-in -practice/tracing-the-trickle-down-in-roman -recycling.

Edelson, Mat. "Arsenic in Swann Park." *John Hopkins Public Health Magazine*, Fall 2007. https:/ /magazine.jhsph.edu/2007/fall/features/swann _park.

Ehrlich, Anne, and Paul Ehrlich. "Ecoscience: The Greeks and Romans Did it, Too!" *Mother Earth News*, May/Jun 1980. https://www .motherearthnews.com/nature-and-environment /greeks-and-romans-zmaz80mjzraw.

Fears, Darryl. "Within Mainstream Environmentalist Groups, Diversity is Lacking." *Washington Post,* March 24, 2013. https://www.washingtonpost .com.

Ferruccio, Deborah. "'A Fierce Green Fire' Applies to Warren Co." Warren Record, February 19, 2014. http://www.warrenrecord.com/opinion /article_2706bc90-996b-11e3-acba -001a4bcf887a.html.

Granados, Alex, and Frank Stasio. "Meet Deborah and Ken Ferruccio." WUNC.org, October 24, 2011. http://wunc.org/post/meet -deborah-and-ken-ferruccio#stream/0.

Griffin, Kevin. "This Week in History: Banning CFCs and Saving the Ozone layer Took a Global Effort." *Vancouver Sun*, December 30, 2016. http://vancouversun.com/news/local -news/this-week-in-history-banning-cfcs-and -saving-the-ozone-layer-took-a-global-effort.

Klein, Naomi. *This Changes Everything: Capital-*

ism vs. the Climate. New York, NY: Simon & Schuster, 2014.

Klein, Naomi. "Time for Big Green to go Fossil-Free." Nation, May 1, 2013. https://www .thenation.com/article/time-big-green-go-fossil -free.

McKenna, Phil. "Environmental Justice Grabs a Megaphone in the Climate Movement." *Inside Climate News*, January 5, 2018. https:// insideclimatenews.org.

Pereira, Sydney. NASA: Hole in Earth's Ozone Layer Finally Closing Up Because Humans Did Something About It." *Newsweek*, January 5, 2018. http://www.newsweek.com/nasa -hole-earths-ozone-layer-finally-closing-humans -did-something-771922.

Reed, Susan, and Lorenzo Benet. "Eco-Warrior Dave Foreman Will Do Whatever it Takes in his Fight to Save Mother Earth." *People*, April 16, 1990. http://people.com/archive/eco-warrior -dave-foreman-will-do-whatever-it-takes-in-his -fight-to-save-mother-earth-vol-33-no-15.

Skelton, Renee, and Vernice Miller. "The Environmental Justice Movement." *Natural Resources Defense Council*, March 17, 2016. https://www .nrdc.org/stories/environmental-justice -movement.

Skilling, Tom. "Dear Tom, Who Coined the Word Smog?" *Chicago Tribune*, January 11, 2003.

http://articles.chicagotribune.com/2003-01-11
/news/0301110089_1_smog-fog-pollution.

Speth, James. "Environmental Failure: A Case for
a New Green Politics." Yale Environment 360,
October 20, 2008. https://e360.yale.edu
/features/environmental_failure_a_case_for_a
_new_green_politics.

United States Environmental Protection Agency.
"History of the Clean Water Act." Retrieved
March 16, 2018. https://www.epa.gov/laws
-regulations/history-clean-water-act.

U.S. Department of Energy. "Environmental Justice History." Retrieved March 15, 2018. https://
www.energy.gov/lm/services/environmental
-justice/environmental-justice-history.

Weyler, Rex. "A Brief History of Environmentalism."
Greenpeace.org, January 5, 2018. https://www
.greenpeace.org/archive-international/en/news
/Blogs/makingwaves/a-brief-history-of
-environmentalism/blog/60967.

INDEX

ABOUT THE AUTHOR

Philip Wolny is a writer and editor hailing from Queens, New York. He lives in New York with his wife and daughter. He has written numerous young-adult educational titles on a wide array of topics, including social movements and protest, extreme weather, science, and more. Some of his titles include *Food Supply Collapse* (Doomsday Scenarios: Separating Fact from Fiction), *Everything You Need to Know About Protests and Public Assembly* (The Need to Know Library), *Write Like a Scientist*, and *Native American Treatment and Resistance*.

PHOTO CREDITS